TEAMWORK

While people often think of teamwork only in terms of sports teams, it is present in many other aspects of life too.

THE LEARNING-A-LIVING LIBRARY

High Performance Through
TEAMWORK

Bob Gartner

THE ROSEN PUBLISHING GROUP, INC.
NEW YORK

Published in 1996 by The Rosen Publishing Group, Inc.
29 East 21st Street, New York, NY 10010

First Edition

Printed in the United States of America

Library of Congress Cataloging-in-Publication Data

Gartner, Bob.
    Teamwork / Bob Gartner.
        p.   cm. — (The learning-a-living library)
    Includes bibliographical references and index.
    Summary: Discusses teamwork skills and their usefulness in school,
at work, and in a future career.
    ISBN 0-8239-2209-X
    1. Work groups—Juvenile literature.   [1. Work groups.]
I. Title.   II. Series.
HD66.G377   1996
658.3'128—dc20   95-39725
                                                                    CIP
                                                                     AC

Contents

Introduction

NICOLE'S TEAM TRAILED BY TWO POINTS WITH FIVE seconds remaining in the opening basketball game of the season. She wanted to do something to help her team win.

Seeing her chance, Nicole cut in front of the opposing forward to intercept the pass. Her teammate Amy broke free and was all alone under the basket.

Instead of passing to Amy, Nicole started dribbling toward the basket. A pass to Amy for an easy layup ties the game and sends it into overtime, she thought. A three-point basket wins the game.

At the three-point line she stopped and shot. She scored! Her team had a one-point win. In the stands, the crowd exploded in a victory cheer. Nicole's excited teammates embraced her.

No one noticed the referees conferring at the official scorer's table. Amid the celebration, the public address announcer informed the crowd that time had expired before Nicole's shot: The basket didn't count. Defeat replaced victory. The jubilant stood in stunned disbelief.

Later, after the reality of the loss had sunk in, the coach asked Nicole why she hadn't passed the ball to Amy, who was alone under the basket and could have tied the game. "I saw Amy, but I knew I could make the shot and win the game," explained Nicole. The coach was patient. "Basketball is a team game, Nicole," he said. "The letter 'I' does not appear in the spelling of Team. We win when we help each other and play as a team. When we play as individuals, we look disorganized and rarely win. Look to your teammates for help, and don't try to win the game by yourself."

One of the most valuable lessons a coach can teach players is, "Look to your teammates for help." The advice applies not only to sports but to other aspects of life. This book illustrates teamwork in school life and how teamwork skills can further your progress in the world of work.

The workplace is putting increased emphasis on teamwork. Companies are using employee teams to solve problems, design new products, and plan for future growth. As you become a team member and interact with your teammates, sharing your skills and learning skills from them, remember the coach's advice, "Look to your teammates for help."

In the workplace, an increasing number of companies are using employee teams to accomplish goals more efficiently.

Teamwork Is Everywhere

WHAT EXACTLY IS TEAMWORK? TEAMWORK IS A cooperative or coordinated effort by a group of people acting together for a common cause. A team is a group of people who pool their experience, skills, and knowledge to work on a common task for which they hold themselves and each other responsible. In these definitions of teamwork and team, "common" means that all the members are working on or for the same purpose or goal.

Teamwork is usually identified with sports. Soccer, football, basketball, hockey, rowing, baseball, and lacrosse are examples of team sports. In team sports, a group of players depend upon each other as they work together toward a common goal: victory. In individual sports like tennis, wrestling, or bowling, the individual's skills are on display as the person triumphs or fails.

In team sports, an individual's contribution is often obscured by the action of the game. Even if a team has an exceptional player, that player still

Firefighters work in teams to combat a blaze quickly and effectively.

needs the whole team's effort to be successful. The sports world is full of examples of teams that fail to perform successfully even though the team owners assembled as many "superstars" as possible. When the teams fail to win, bad "chemistry" is blamed. The stars are not able or willing to blend their skills toward the overall goal of team victory.

Although we often think of sports when teamwork is mentioned, look around as you go through a day and you will see examples of teamwork that you take for granted.

When you see firefighters battling a burning

building, you might think that all they do is spray water on the fire. Actually, each member of the crew has an assigned job. From the moment they arrive at the scene, one team makes sure that the building is empty while another team unrolls and hooks up the hoses to the hydrants. The leaders quickly estimate the strength and direction of the fire and decide where to attack it. Water is not just sprayed onto a building. The firefighters may attack the head of the fire while also wetting down areas in front of it so that the fire won't be able to spread there. Firefighters are well trained in teamwork because every minute wasted could cost lives.

Marching bands spend hours practicing formations until all the members move together as one. The bands usually work up new routines throughout the season. Typically, they receive new music and formation on a Monday and practice the rest of the week for a Friday or Saturday performance. Similar to marching bands are choral groups and orchestras. Every musical note has to be perfectly blended.

A stock car racing pit crew practices pit stops until each movement is automatic. Only seven people are allowed over the pit road wall when a car comes in for gas and a tire change. The jack man uses a special hydraulic jack to raise one side of the car. Two tire changers use automatic lug wrenches to remove the driver's front and back tires on one side and install new ones. Two other members lift new tires over the wall and exchange them for the old tires. The gas man plunges the nozzle of a 15-gallon gas can into the tank. Another team member holds a container near a special overflow tube to catch any spilled gas. The seventh person goes over the wall only if the car is having mechanical problems. From behind the wall he cleans the driver's windshield with a long-handled squeegee.

A good pit crew can change two tires and gas the car in under 20 seconds. The majority of stock car races are closely contested, with the winner sometimes having a .1-second margin of victory. Veteran race observers frequently say that "races are won or lost in the pits," meaning that a fast pit stop can provide the margin of victory and a slow stop can lose a race. To be effective and help their driver win, the pit crew must work as a team.

National Park Service rangers form rescue teams in the national parks and rehearse rescue situations. Yosemite National Park in California attracts thousands of mountain and rock climbers. Unfortunately, not all of these climbers are experienced, and many get into dangerous situations. Yosemite averages 125 to 150 rescue missions each year. Rangers with an interest in mountain climbing are drawn to the mountainous parks like Yosemite,

Examples of teamwork can be found throughout the animal kingdom.

Rocky Mountain, Grand Canyon, Grand Teton, and Yellowstone, where they sharpen their skills for use in rescue missions. The rescue teams get together after work to practice climbing and simulate rescues. New team members are brought along slowly until they are fully prepared.

Teamwork extends even to the animal kingdom. Have you ever seen geese fly in their familiar V-shaped formation? When geese fly in formation they travel about 70 percent faster than when they fly alone. When the lead goose tires, it drops back into the "V" and another goose moves forward to become the leader. If a sick or weak goose drops out of the formation, at least one other goose also drops out to help and protect the ailing goose.

Animals like wolves and lions use teamwork when they hunt. Five or six female lions hunt together. They approach a grazing herd of wildebeest, spread out in a line, and stalk the herd, moving only when they are unobserved. The lions at the ends of the line advance more quickly than those in the center and pinch the wildebeest toward the center. When the lions on the flank are detected, or when they charge, the herd bolts and the flankers drive some of the wildebeest toward the lions in the center of the line.

Teamwork is all around you: at home, at school, at work. Meeting with a group of friends to study for tests or organizing an event with an after-school club are examples of teamwork in school. In a part-time job, you're probably not running the place yourself; you no doubt depend on the efforts of your coworkers and the guidance of your boss. Teamwork is an important part of your future, too. Sure, you're becoming more independent, but working well with others is one of the things that will help you make it on your own. Employers notice employees who are "team players." Working well with groups of people is a skill you will need your whole life.

By being part of a team, we can accomplish

much more, much faster than we could working alone. Author Alexandre Dumas, who wrote *The Three Musketeers*, probably stated the first motto of teamwork with the Musketeers' slogan: "All for one and one for all."

A more modern but less catchy motto, offered by James L. Lundy in his book *Teams: How to Develop Peak Performance Teams for World-Class Results*, is:

T ogether
E ach
A chieves
M ore
S uccess!

Questions to Ask Yourself

Although teamwork is usually identified with sports, there are examples of teamwork surrounding you every day. 1) What are some examples of teamwork that you encounter in your daily life? How do they affect your life? 2) What are some of the benefits of working as a team? Why are team efforts usually more effective than individual efforts? 3) What kinds of animals use teamwork?

Families often work as a team, splitting up different tasks among members.

Teamwork at Home and School

FAMILY AND SCHOOL ARE OUR EARLIEST introductions to cooperation with others, which leads to teamwork. Most families operate by teamwork, with everyone pitching in wherever help is needed. Teamwork is especially important in single-parent families in which the parent is working one or two jobs. Much of the burden of housekeeping falls to the oldest child, who becomes responsible for the younger children until the parent comes home. Everyone, even the youngest child, has to contribute and share the work. As the children grow older, their roles change and their contributions increase.

Family Teamwork

Families work out a system for sharing household tasks. But family teamwork is not only about work around the house. Planning a vacation or an outing can become a teamwork opportunity. For a vacation, each member can research some aspect of the

Families, like other kinds of teams, should communicate often. Family meetings are a good way to keep lines of communication open.

proposed site such as restaurants, tourist attractions, historical sites, motels, or the driving route. All members should let the others know what they really want from this vacation. The family can meet once a week for a progress report and make decisions as they are needed.

Other examples of family teamwork are planning a birthday party, organizing a daily schedule for transporting everyone to or from their various activities, or entertaining company with everyone helping in the planning and preparation of dinner.

Teamwork is evident when open communication helps family members to understand one another.

In families where people respect one another, the family members support and encourage each other's efforts and achievements. Most of us participate in teamwork within our own family, even if we don't realize it.

Teams in School

School projects are perfect for helping students learn how to work together. A number of school districts use "cooperative learning" strategies. As a team, the students discuss what they need and help each other gather information. They review their material and prepare a team presentation for the rest of the class. They are graded as a team, and the teams compete against one another. By working cooperatively, helping each other and being helped, sharing ideas, and competing against the other teams, the students learn teamwork.

For example, a history teacher divides students into teams of four. Their assignment is to put together a presentation on a U.S. president. First, the students select the president they will report on. They decide that one student will gather information on the president's early life. Another will research the presidential campaign. Another will report on the presidency. The fourth student will research the lasting effects and outcomes of the presidency. After researching their own topics, the

Studying for tests as a group can be a helpful way to exchange ideas and improve individual performance.

students come together to decide what material will be included in the presentation. They might appoint a leader to present their work to the class, or they might take turns speaking.

Whenever they are faced with a difficult subject or an involved project, students find it helps to form teams, dividing the workload and then sharing their research. Self-designed study groups are popular with law school and medical students, where the amount of information to be learned is overwhelming.

School provides a wide variety of opportunities to work cooperatively and learn teamwork. Examples are school newspapers and yearbooks, clubs, orchestra, singing groups, sports teams, debate teams, and student government.

School plays often involve large numbers of students. Most of the attention centers on the performers, but student teams oversee stage design and set construction, lighting, sound, and makeup. The students working on these teams never get curtain calls or applause, but their contributions are essential to the success of the production.

Questions to Ask Yourself

Family and school are two early introductions to teamwork. Learning how to cooperate and combine efforts at home and school can benefit you in the future. 1) How does your family work as a team to keep everything running smoothly? 2) In what ways do teachers have their students work in teams? 3) What are some ways in which you could use teamwork to increase performance after school—in activities or when studying?

Teamwork on the Job

In Chapter 1 we found that teamwork is widespread, even though we often don't notice it. The same is also true of the workplace. When you enter the workplace, you will realize that few jobs require no help from others.

The life of a writer seems independent, but the writer interviews people for information, uses libraries and online information services, and works with the editor of the publishing house to turn the manuscript into a book. The editor works with the publicity department to spread news about the book, and with the sales representatives to prepare them to recommend it to their customers. For a book or an author that the publisher considers important, the publicity department arranges for the author to make a book tour, visiting potential sales outlets and giving interviews on television and radio. The author and the publisher work as a team to bring the book to print and assure its sales.

Teachers also work in teams. They share infor-

Even jobs that seem independent involve teamwork in some way. A writer, for example, may need to work with library staff to get the information she needs.

It's OK to disagree with teammates, as long as your criticism is offered in a constructive way.

mation on subjects and techniques, and help each other to improve the quality of the education you receive. Teachers also interact as a team with school administrators and students. Some schools encourage team teaching, with two or more teachers instructing the class.

When you enter the workplace, you will be helping others and depending on others. You may not immediately be involved in a formal team concept, but you will be part of some form of team. If you are put on a team early in your career, don't panic.

You were selected because of your skills and abilities, and you are expected to use your talents to help the team reach its goal. Your role is to be a contributing member.

Alec is a busperson at a busy restaurant. He knows that he works as a team with his fellow employees. He and the waitress, Tara, rely on each others' signals. He needs to clear the appetizer dishes before she serves the salads. He removes the salad plates as Tara serves the main course. When he takes away the main course dishes, Tara knows it's time to ask if the customers would like dessert. Back in the kitchen, Alex relies on the dishwasher, Matt, to have clean water glasses and silverware ready for him to set the tables. He depends on Jody, the kitchen assistant, to have bread baskets ready, just as she relies on him to tell her how many more she should make. In this sort of fast-paced environment, good teamwork is critical. It makes sense that restaurant employees often split the servers' tips among the rest of the staff.

Some of your team members may be heads of departments or vice-presidents, but try not to be overwhelmed by their positions. You are all there to achieve a specific goal, and everyone on the team is equal, even the team leader.

As a team member, you have an obligation to the team to do the best job possible. You have that same obligation to yourself and your employer throughout your career. By embracing the team concept and exerting that extra effort, you will bring yourself to the attention of the management people on the team. You may find yourself placed on the fast track for promotions and increased responsibilities.

Questions to Ask Yourself

Almost every kind of job requires employees to work together to accomplish different goals. Working together, employees are able to finish tasks quickly and effectively. 1) If you have a job, who is your team leader? In what ways does he or she require you to work with others? 2) What kind of team skills have you developed at home or school that you could apply to your job? 3) How does a busy restaurant use teamwork to maintain quick service?

Teams and Teamwork

WHY DO SOME TEAMS SUCCEED WHILE OTHERS
fail? Both success and failure have many causes.
Let's examine some of the qualities of a successful
team. Remember the definition: a group of people
who pool their experience, skills, and knowledge to
work on a common task for which they hold themselves and each other responsible.

Most successful teams are small, usually between
two and twenty-five members. Smaller is better.
The ideal size is six to eight members. Teams with
more than twenty-five members often have trouble
interacting in a useful way. Such groups usually
form smaller teams rather than acting as a single team.

The most important principle of the team is a
clear understanding of its goal. Every member must
know why the team was formed and what it is expected to accomplish. When every member under-
stands the goal, the members are likely to make
better contributions toward it. Knowing the goal
also helps team members to feel greater satisfaction
in their effort.

A school orchestra relies on the conductor to direct groups of instruments.

Once the goal is understood, team members need to decide how they will work together. The team must decide who will do particular jobs, how schedules will be set, and how the team will make decisions. These ground rules are important so that all members know their roles and responsibilities on the team.

Team Leadership

When the team first meets, they should select a leader. Sometimes the team leader is appointed by a company's management. The leader's role is to keep the team focused on the goal and guide it to high performance. The leader must believe in the importance of the goal, and that each person can make a valuable contribution toward it. Team leaders deal with problems, resolve conflicts, and keep the team moving toward its goal. A leader should work to build the commitment and confidence of each member as well as the team as a whole.

Everyone on a team, including the leader, does work in equal amounts. The team leader contributes just like any other member. When "dirty work" is required, the team leader should step forward. An example of "dirty work" is telling a company's management that there are problems, and that the team is exploring other ideas. No one wants to go before the bosses with bad news, but that responsibility belongs to the team leader.

Part of being an effective team leader is a willingness to share recognition and praise and to shoulder the blame if something goes wrong. A team will have trouble working together if the leader takes the credit for successes and blames the team members for failure.

"We" Thinking

Recently, an officer in the army was promoted to the rank of colonel. He had led a team to streamline regulations on purchasing supplies for army bases in the United States. The team was able to eliminate hundreds of pages of confusing and contradictory regulations. The team also made recommendations for speeding the purchase of supplies and the payment of suppliers, many whom had to wait six months or more to be paid. The colonel personally thanked each member of his team for helping the team achieve success. At his promotion ceremony, he introduced the team and said, "I am the one receiving the award, but any success I have achieved is due to their efforts."

Even if they don't receive awards, each team member has a responsibility to work for the success of the team. This means making your best personal contribution. Teamwork can fulfill the desire for

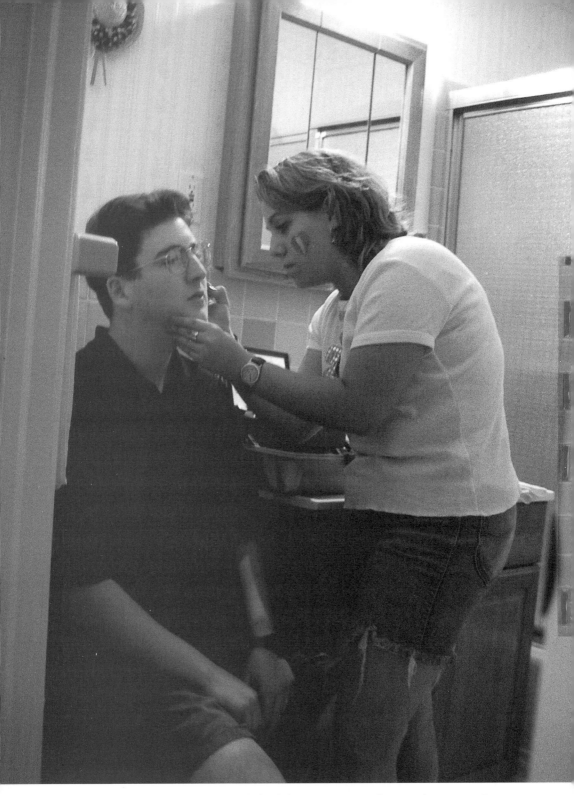

Applying makeup is one of many "behind the scenes" team elements that go into the production of a school play.

community and belonging. As a team member, you think in terms of "we." "We" are working. "We" are accomplishing. It is "our" work, "our" product. With that attitude, the team members demonstrate the Three Musketeers' motto: All for one and one for all.

Strength Through Diversity

Teams are usually made up of people with different skills or backgrounds. The intent is to bring together a variety of skills to solve a problem, design a product, or plan a strategy.

If a team is formed to produce a new car, it would be a disaster to have only designers on the team. The team would have to include people from marketing, engineering, production, sales, parts, and labor. Each person would be able to contribute information on how much the car would cost to make; how long it would take to produce it; what features are popular on cars and what the buying public is demanding; whether parts would be available for the new car; how much time manufacturers would need to supply parts; how much labor is involved, and what labor-saving and cost-saving machinery could be used.

When Chrysler decided to build a sports car to compete with Chevrolet's Corvette, they brought together a team of more than forty of their brightest designers, engineers, manufacturing specialists, and managers.

Then, Chrysler turned the team loose and let them use whoever and whatever they needed from the company. The result was the Dodge Viper, a $54,000 sports car with a top speed of 160 mph. The car became an immediate hit and gave Chrysler's image a much-needed boost.

Setting Objectives

On the way to the goal, a team should determine a set of objectives to be met and a time schedule for meeting them. Objectives are similar to goals. They are definite steps that need to be accomplished on the way to reaching the goal. Progress toward the objectives should be measured on a regular basis.

Teams need successes to keep people excited about their work. When a goal is reached, the team should celebrate. Teams need recognition for the same reasons individuals do. In the early going, recognition makes the team feel good and motivates the members. As the team becomes established, the members can decide on ways of recognizing individual members for high performance and congratulating the whole team for a job well done.

A Period of Adjustment

When a team is formed, whether in sports, in

school, or in the workplace, there is bound to be a time in the early going when the team does not function smoothly. This is expected as members learn their roles and adapt to their new teammates.

Have you ever watched a soccer team of six- or seven-year-olds? In the first few games, they look like a swarm of bees moving across the field after the ball. By the third or fourth game, however, the players begin to get the idea of how the game should be played, and some strategy starts to emerge. They are learning plays and how to pass the ball, and they're getting to know each other. Sometimes they even score a goal. As the season continues, the swarm of bees begins to spread out and play as a team. They may not win many games, but they've learned teamwork.

Questions to Ask Yourself

For a team to be successful, it must have certain important qualities. Answer these questions to test your knowledge of good teamwork. 1) What are some of the characteristics of an effective team? Why are such characteristics beneficial? 2) Why must every team have a leader? Who are some team leaders in your activities? 3) What are some ways in which a team can keep morale and motivation levels high?

Team Dynamics: The Four Stages

TEAM DYNAMICS REFERS TO THE DEVELOPMENT stages through which a team progresses and the continual interaction between members. As mentioned earlier, teams experience a shakedown period during which members become comfortable with each other, determine the team goals and their individual roles, and begin to perform. Researchers identify four stages of team development: forming, storming, norming, and performing. Let's briefly examine each stage.

Stage 1: Forming. Forming is also known as Orientation. The team members are just meeting each other and are very polite and careful not to offend other members. They are not sure why they are on the team but are still eager to be in the group. At this stage, the members are dependent on the leader. Their effectiveness as a team is low because they haven't worked together. The team would flounder without the leader, who makes their purpose and goal clear, keeps them on course, and assigns work.

Team members have to overcome problems such as conflicting personalities if the team is to work together.

Stage 2: Storming. This stage is also known as Dissatisfaction and is characterized by a dip in morale because trust and confidence have not yet been established. This is the most challenging stage. The atmosphere is often emotionally charged as team members disagree about how to reach the goal. More aggressive members can overpower the quieter members. Certain members may be blamed for the problem that the team is being asked to solve. Conflict then develops and the team feels stuck in a rut.

At this stage, members need to encourage each other to talk about their feelings. Open communication is essential if the team is to move to the next stage.

The leader spends more time offering praise and support for the members. A skillful leader moves the team toward the third stage by speaking honestly, listening actively, encouraging participation, and helping members understand the contributions of other members.

Stage 3: Norming. Also called the Resolution stage, this occurs when the group begins to build an identity. Members put aside their self-interests and instead work for the benefit of the team and its goals. They begin to value each other's opinions and contributions and become tolerant of differences. This is the stage at which the ground rules are usually set. The goals are clarified, and the team learns how to confront issues, resolve conflicts, set schedules, and develop their skills. Dependence on the leader decreases. The leader's role is to be supportive as the team becomes more confident and moves toward the final stage.

Stage 4: Performing. This stage, also called Production, is characterized by strong skills on one hand and commitment on the other. Morale is high. The members feel appreciated and involved. They have learned to be tolerant of individual weaknesses and to utilize strengths. The team has a thorough understanding of goals and a high level of performance. They have learned to take advantage of the knowledge of each team member. Openness and trust prevail in meetings. Members are relaxed, flexible, and supportive of each other. Problems that used to cause trouble for the group are now easily handled.

Performing teams are ready for self-management. They need little direction or support from the leader. Although the leader still runs the meetings and monitors the team's performance, the leader can surrender that role as other members assume some leadership. Once the team gains a reputation for high performance, they are often asked to take on new tasks.

In some cases, the team members seem to mesh

Synergy is achieved when a team's efforts exceed the sum of the efforts of its members. It is the highest level of team performance.

perfectly. Their performance as a group is greater than the contribution of any one member or the sum of all the members. When this happens, the team has achieved "synergy". The whole is greater than the sum of its parts, and teamwork becomes spectacular.

Synergy requires each member to contribute and to respect the contribution of other members. Synergy happens when concern for the team's goal is combined with trust and mutual support among the members.

It is important for a team to celebrate once a goal has been achieved. This gives the team an opportunity to relax before beginning new projects.

Synergy in Action

Let's look at an example of synergy and the four stages of teamwork dynamics. A computer company forms a team because the company has a poor reputation for customer service. The team goal is to determine the causes of the poor reputation and recommend ways to rebuild it. The team consists of five people, the department heads from customer service, sales, technical development, finance, and employee training. In the Forming stage, each member thinks he or she knows the reason for the poor reputation.

During the Storming stage, each member feels that the goal may be unattainable, and that other departments are to blame for the problem. Customer service believes that the sales people are promising more than their computers are capable of doing. Sales believes that the technical manuals are so poorly written that the customers can't understand them. The technical development head thinks that employees, particularly the sales people, are not trained well enough to sell the computers. The training head thinks that finance doesn't put aside enough money for training. Finance has a budget to meet and wants to keep costs down.

As the team moves into the Norming stage, the members have investigated their departments and talked to customers. Accusations of blame and pointing of fingers have stopped. They are listening to one another and examining each other's points. The goal is to identify and correct any false information or assumptions. The members contradict and challenge one another, but in an open and honest way. Everyone is involved and committed. Morale is high because they believe they are on the way to solving the problem. They are no longer worried about their particular department's reputation. Their concern is for the company's reputation.

The team moves into the Performing stage and starts working on solutions. The technical department will write a new user-friendly manual for customers and revise the technical manual for the customer service staff. The finance head has examined the company's budget and found funding for the changes in the manual and new training programs for the sales force. The customer service head has streamlined the approach to customer problems and put together a same-day response policy. Because of these improvements, the sales staff has stronger selling points. The team thinks that these improvements can be in place within twelve months and commits to that deadline.

This is synergistic teamwork. Each member learned something from the others: an understanding of what the other departments did. The team's understanding of the situation is far beyond each individual's understanding of the problem when the team was formed. Instead of blaming each other for the company's poor reputation, the team members saw that there were problems in many departments. When a team has synergy, they feel that they can accomplish anything.

Questions to Ask Yourself

Team dynamics refers to the stages through which a team progresses and the way in which its members interact. 1) What are the four stages of team dynamics? 2) What occurs during the storming phase? How can a team move successfully from this stage to norming? 3) Have you ever been on a team that achieved synergy? What were the results of this achievement?

Why Some Teams Fail

NOT ALL GROUPS OF PEOPLE THAT TRY TO work together become teams. Groups become teams when the members recognize a common goal, listen to one another, resolve conflicts, make decisions with group input, and adopt the "we" and "our" attitude.

What can be done to prevent teams from crashing? Among the many reasons for a team's failure, these are the primary three:

1. Teams that fail usually haven't developed a common goal. The members are not sure of their roles or responsibilities or why the team was formed. Without a common goal, some members lose their commitment, or they are asked to do things for which they lack the skills or training. Without a commitment to the team, a person probably won't be a happy or productive team member.

2. Members don't communicate or handle conflict. Problems arise when team members fail to

speak openly or truthfully. Rather than bring out their concerns at a meeting, members may complain to other members or outsiders away from the team setting. Once gossip starts, relationships go downhill fast.

The team may be made up of people who are described by their coworkers as "very effective" or "excellent." When effective individuals interact, however, they may or may not produce an effective team. Sloppy standards, unclear goals, personal dislikes, and disagreements may interfere with the group becoming a team. Team performance is productive only if the members have the "we" and "our" attitude.

During the ground-rules session, shortly after a team is formed, the team must work out the best ways to raise issues, resolve problems, and move on with the required work.

3. Members have difficult personal styles. Hidden behind disruptive behavior may be a desire for attention and recognition.

The personal work habits of members can cause problems. One member dislikes morning meetings, whereas another doesn't want to meet after lunch. One member wants to take coffee breaks; another prefers to continue without breaks. Some members think that they are doing more work than others. These seem like minor obstacles and should be

Take the time to get to know your fellow teammates. By increasing your familiarity with each other, you can improve the team's performance.

easily handled in the Norming session when ground rules are set. If they are not dealt with early on, however, they become major roadblocks. If team members learn to deal with behavior without creating more arguments, they can help the individual build self-esteem and enable the team to move forward.

It often helps a group to begin a meeting by stating that the original reason for forming the team was to use—not ignore—different individual styles. It is the variety of team members' strengths, education, work experiences, problem-solving skills, and points of view that makes teams a powerful idea.

What happens when one member is not "pulling his weight"? Recognize that it may simply be a misunderstanding. A team leader can talk with the team member and try to understand how that person views the team and his role in it. Sometimes, clarifying what is expected is enough to reunify the whole team. It may be that some other problem exists. Talking about it might resolve it. If not, or if the person does not want to be a part of the team, the best solution may be to let him go and bring in a new team member.

Letting someone go need not be regarded as a defeat for the team. Disruptive or unwilling team members can make things unpleasant for everyone else. By addressing members' concerns and keeping communication open, the well-being of the team and its individual members can be maintained.

Questions to Ask Yourself

There are a number of reasons why certain teams fail to accomplish their goals. Recognizing the warning signs can help your team avoid failure. 1) What are the three primary reasons why teams fail? 2) What are some examples of disruptive personal styles? 3) How might a team deal with an uncooperative team member?

Interpersonal Relationship Guidelines

WHAT SKILLS DO YOU NEED AS YOU SEEK A JOB and enter the workforce? The U.S. Secretary of Labor formed the Secretary's Commission on Achieving Necessary Skills (SCANS) to determine the skills that young adults need to succeed in the world of work. Their report, released in 1992, listed five skills that young workers need for solid job performance. One of the required skills is interpersonal skills, defined as the ability to work on teams, teach others, serve customers, lead, negotiate, and work well with people from different cultural backgrounds.

Interpersonal skills—the way you relate to and deal with other people—are essential for good teamwork. Following are some guidelines for building good interpersonal relationships with your team members. Beyond the team, these guidelines will help you in your daily interactions with your family, coworkers, customers, and friends.

- Try to be cheerful and friendly. Try to maintain a positive attitude, and see if you can find any good even in a difficult situation. This does not mean that you need to have a smile on your face at all times. But an upbeat attitude usually attracts people and makes even stressful times more bearable.
- Try to treat others with respect. Remember that they too have concerns about their own self-esteem and recognition. Ask them about their ideas, their families, and their plans. Express interest. Treat others as you want to be treated.
- Maintain a calm manner. How you say something is sometimes more important than what you say. If you lose your temper and shout or threaten, people will remember your actions but not what you said. Remember your ABCs— Always Be Cool.
- Try to listen as well as speak. Everyone wants to be heard, just as you do. After all, most people enjoy being with others who listen to them. By keeping your ears open to what others have to say, you can learn many new and interesting things.
- Keep others informed in a positive way. Share your insights into possible challenges (problems should be considered challenges) and opportunities. Don't make promises. When you do make a

The art of communication involves being a good listener.

commitment, be sure to keep it. Let your word be your bond.

- Avoid spreading rumors and negative comments about others. Don't participate in talking behind other people's backs. We've all seen how gossip and rumors can damage a person's reputation. Look at people who enjoy spreading negative comments. Do they seem happy to you? Spend your time building good relationships rather than tearing them down.
- Be flexible. On a team, you need to adjust your individual preferences, priorities, and workstyle in

order to work smoothly with others. Being stubborn is harmful to good teamwork. Loosen up, adapt to new situations, and both you and the team will benefit.

- Maintain a balance between constructive criticism and praise. When criticizing someone's work or ideas, do so in a positive way. Look for the good points and comment on them while bringing the person back on track in a constructive manner. Look for opportunities to give praise. Everyone can learn from constructive criticism, and no one wants to hear negative things about their efforts.
- Keep an open mind and avoid defensiveness. You can disagree without being disagreeable. You don't have to win every argument. Look at the other person's point of view and find a mutual understanding. A defensive person closes his mind to another's viewpoint, resulting in arguments and conflict.

An important part of teamwork is suggesting ideas—brainstorming. Members look at a problem and suggest various solutions. Some are eliminated; some are kept for further discussion until one idea is selected and developed as the best solution. If your idea is not selected this time, it may be next time. Don't be discouraged; stay involved even if another idea is chosen, because you may be able to improve it. Your input is always valuable.

- Remember that you can accomplish much more when you don't care who gets the credit. In teamwork, credit goes to the team rather than individual members. This is the "we" and "our" attitude; the team's concern is producing an outstanding product, not who gets the glory. If an individual is singled out for praise, that person should show that he or she wants to share the rewards and spotlight with the team.

Questions to Ask Yourself

All teams have people with different personalities. Because there will always be different kinds of people on a team, it is important to develop good interpersonal skills. 1) Do you recognize any of the interpersonal skills mentioned as characteristic of your relationships with others? 2) What are some of the practices that help communication? Why are they so important? 3) How can brainstorming improve a team's performance?

Teamwork and Your Career

AS BUSINESSES AND GOVERNMENT EXAMINE themselves, they are realizing that their employees are their most important resource. Smart employers are using the energy of their people. The workplace of the '90s is moving away from the structure of having a small group of managers directing everyone. The traditional roles of management and labor are being replaced by partnerships. At many companies, employees are not only encouraged to become involved and contribute their ideas; they're also being empowered to make decisions and manage their own jobs. Companies that empower their workers realize that people are more excited to start and complete those things that they have helped create.

Total Quality Management

In the past, American companies were the leaders in producing and supplying the world with goods and services. Today, the situation has changed. As other countries have increased their industrial output, the United States has expanded its service-oriented businesses. In the effort to stay competitive, some leaders in business and government are trying new approaches to management. One approach is Total Quality Management or TQM.

The concept of TQM was developed by an American professor, W. Edwards Deming, in the 1940s. The Japanese used his management principles to rebuild their country after World War II and move them to a leadership role in the world economy. TQM is characterized by an increased focus on customer requirements, teamwork, and employees. Customers want quality products and services delivered on time. To accomplish this, some businesses and governments are now enabling the workers who are involved with producing goods and delivering services to analyze and improve the way they do their jobs. In the past, analysis and improvement were the responsibility of management. TQM includes involvement, empowerment, commitment, and partnership of employees with management. Teams and teamwork are key elements of TQM.

More and more companies are finding that teamwork means better performance in industry. Teams and teamwork are leading efforts to increase the sales of industrial products.

This is the workplace that you will be entering.

The concept of Total Quality Management is designed to help employees feel committed to their jobs.

Teams and teamwork will play a central role in your career. Teamwork is the organizational structure of the future.

Questions to Ask Yourself

Teamwork will almost certainly be an aspect of your future career. Many companies are using unique teamwork applications to achieve higher levels of success. 1) Why was TQM created? 2) Who developed the concept of TQM and where did he get his ideas? 3) What are the key elements of TQM?

Glossary

autonomous Capable of existing independently.

brainstorming Method of generating ideas. A group "storms" a problem with their brains, producing ideas that are listed and later examined in detail.

competent Having the necessary ability or qualities.

diversity Differences.

empowerment Giving of power or authority.

goal The result or achievement toward which effort is directed.

ground rules Rules of procedure; a guide on how to interact.

interpersonal Pertaining to the relations between persons.

objective The desired result to be achieved within a specific time period.

plan Course of action designed to attain a stated objective.

problem Question or situation proposed for solution.

skill Ability to use one's knowledge effectively and readily in completing a task.

strategy Broad course of action, chosen from a number of alternatives, to accomplish a stated goal.

synergy The action of two or more events or things to achieve an effect which neither could achieve individually.

task Assigned piece of work to be finished within a certain time.

Organizations

ONE OF THE BEST WAYS TO GET EXPERIENCE IN teamwork is to join a club or organization that is of special interest to you. Do you enjoy acting? If you do, join the drama club at school. If you like to fish, try an organization like Trout Unlimited (TU) or Bass Anglers Sportsmans Society (BASS). If you are interested in working to save the environment, a number of organizations are available, such as Friends of the Earth, the Sierra Club, or the Rainforest Action Network. Most of these organizations have local chapters.

Joining an organization that interests you is a great way to learn more about your hobby or subject, meet people with the same interests, and gain teamwork experience. If you don't know what organizations you may want to join, explain your interests to the librarian, who can guide you to directories of organizations.

Groups designed for young people interested in business can also be good places to gain teamwork skills, while learning about the world of work. For example:

Business Professionals of America
5454 Clercland Avenue
Columbus, OH 43231

Distributive Education Clubs of America
1908 Association Drive
Reston, VA 22091

Future Business Leaders of America
1912 Association Drive
Reston, VA 22091

Jobs for America's Graduates
1729 King Street
Alexandria, VA 22314

For Further Reading

Blake, Robert R. *Spectacular Teamwork*. New York: John Wiley & Sons Inc., 1987.

Blanchard, Dr. Kenneth. *Building High Performance Teams*. Schaumburg, IL: Video Publishing House & Blanchard Management Company, 1990.

Creech, Bill. *The Five Pillars of TQM*. New York: Truman Talley Books/Dutton, 1994.

Katzenbach, Jon R., and Smith, Douglas K. *The Wisdom of Teams: Creating the High-Performance Organization*. New York: HarperCollins Publishers, Inc., 1994.

Lundy, James L. *How to Develop Peak Performance Teams for World-Class Results*. Chicago: Dartnell Corporation, 1992.

Martin, Don. *TeamThink: Using the Sports Connection to Develop, Motivate, and Manage a Winning Business Team*. New York: Penguin Books USA Inc., 1993.

Wellins, Richard S.; Byham, William C.; and Dixon, George R. *Inside Teams: How 20 World-Class Organizations Are Winning Through Teamwork*. San Francisco, CA: Jossey-Bass Inc., 1994.

Index

About the Author

Bob Gartner is a natural resource specialist and free-lance writer. He lives in Burke, Virginia. He has written articles for outdoor publications, technical journals, and newspapers. This is his third book for young adults.

Photos

Katherine Hsu

Layout and Design

Kim Sonsky